HONEYCOMB

HONEYCOMB

POEMS

CAROL FROST

TRIQUARTERLY BOOKS
NORTHWESTERN UNIVERSITY PRESS

TriQuarterly Books
Northwestern University Press
www.nupress.northwestern.edu

Printed in the United States of America

10 9 8 7 6 5 4 3 2 1

Library of Congress Cataloging-in-Publication Data
Frost, Carol, 1948–
    Honeycomb : poems / Carol Frost.
      p. cm.
    ISBN 978-0-8101-2710-4 (pbk. : alk. paper)
      1. Alzheimer's disease—Poetry. 2. Memory—Poetry. I. Title.
    PS3556.R596H66 2010
    811'.54—dc22

                                                   2010014943

♾ The paper used in this publication meets the minimum requirements of the American National Standard for Information Sciences—Permanence of Paper for Printed Library Materials, ANSI Z39.48-1992.

For Renee Fellner Kydd

and for friends Fiona Dejardin and Terry Slade

The weight of this sad time we must obey;
Speak what we feel, not what we ought to say.
The oldest hath borne most: we that are young,
Shall never see so much, nor live so long.

—*KING LEAR*, ACT 5, SCENE 3

[Bees] extract honey and collect it, a juicy substance remarkable for its extreme sweetness . . . Being neither tame nor wild, so all-powerful is Nature, that . . . she has created a marvel beyond all comparison. What muscular power, what exertion of strength are we in comparison with such vast energy and such industry as theirs?

—PLINY, *NATURAL HISTORY*, BOOK 11, CHAPTER 4

They set about constructing their combs, and forming the wax, or, in other words, making their dwellings and cells; after this they produce their young and then make honey and wax from flowers, and extract bee-glue from the tears of those trees which distil glutinous substances, the juices, gums, and resins, namely of the willow, the elm, and the reed.

—PLINY, *NATURAL HISTORY*, BOOK 11, CHAPTER 5

[Honey] is engendered from the air, mostly at the rising of the constellations . . . , and then just before daybreak. Hence it is, that at early dawn the leaves of trees are found covered with a kind of honeylike dew, and those who go into the open air at that early morning, find their clothes covered, and their hair matted, with a sort of unctuous liquid. Whether . . . it is the sweat of heaven, or whether saliva emanating from the stars, or a juice exuding from the air while purifying itself . . . , falling from so vast a height, attracting corruption in its passage, and tainted by the exhalations of the earth . . . deteriorated besides by the juices of flowers, and then steeped in hives and subjected to such repeated changes—still . . . it affords us by its flavour a most exquisite pleasure, the result, no doubt, of its aethereal nature and origin.

—PLINY, *NATURAL HISTORY*, BOOK 11, CHAPTER 12

CONTENTS

Acknowledgments	xi
(For the ones	3
Pearly flying hair,	5
Abandoned bee boxes piled on each other at meadow end . . .	6
(*Tyrannus tyrannus*)	7
I remember the psychiatrist's exam—	9
Then it was autumn.	10
Two anthills and a late summer hive	11
As if by amber or in Lethe's stream	13
The honeycomb is made from flowers	14
You suddenly wearied. You had to sit	15
Amid a menagerie she sleeps as in a lair—	17
Odor plume, mellifluous humming, thick syrup	18
It was August, it was August	19
If her falling to quiet	20
To live without memory is to have each hour	21
As small lamps drift with river tide	22

Beauty and dust, beauty and dust—   23

All things are taken from us   24

The mind is no tunnel deepening   25

"Generous I may have been, amnesiac   27

Light clear in a window, morning   29

Why are we here who owns this house   30

The humble sense of being alive   31

Pretty to think of the mind at its end   32

She wears geegaws from relatives   33

She saw that the tortured dream wrestled to the floor   34

That was the mind's wild swarm trapezing from an oak limb,   35

When bees sicken a rough   36

She doesn't see herself in the mirror,   37

Fools die every day they live   38

Erring   shoe and sour bib   39

What makes her quiet   41

I watched her sleep then went to the window.   42

Afterword

From the somber deeps horseshoe crabs crawled up on somber shores: 45

ACKNOWLEDGMENTS

The author thanks the editors of the following magazines, where these poems were first published.

Indiana Review:

    "Abandoned bee boxes piled on each other at meadow end . . ."
        (originally published as "Apiary II")

The Kenyon Review:

    "All things are taken from us"

    "Erring   shoe and sour bib"

    "The honeycomb is made from flowers"

Ninth Letter:

    "Pretty to think of the mind at its end" (originally published as "The
        Queen's Desertion")

Ploughshares:

    " 'Generous I may have been, amnesiac" (originally published as
        "Apiary VII")

    "To live without memory is to have each hour" (originally published
        as "Apiary XV")

    "(*Tyrannus tyrannus*)" (originally published as "Two Songs for
        Dementia")

Poetry:

    "(For the ones" (originally published as "Apiary VII")

"From the somber deeps horseshoe crabs crawled up on somber shores:" (originally published as "Man of War")

"The humble sense of being alive" (originally published as "Apiary 40")

Smartish Pace:

"Beauty and dust, beauty and dust—"

TriQuarterly:

"She saw that the tortured dream wrestled to the floor"

"She wears geegaws from relatives"

"That was the mind's wild swarm trapezing from an oak limb,"

"Why are we here who owns this house"

Four poems in this volume were previously published in *The Queen's Desertion* by Carol Frost (TriQuarterly Books/Northwestern University Press, 2006).

HONEYCOMB

(For the ones

who line the corridors and sit

silent in wheelchairs

before the television with the volume off,

whose cares

are small and gray and infinite,

time as ever to be faced . . .

Methuselahs the nurses wash

and dress without haste—

none needed . . .

this one has drunk from the poppy-cup

and drowses in her world of dream. . . .

Heliotrope,

carnations, wakeful violets, and lilies in vases—

masses of flowers—wrap

the urine-and-antiseptic air in lace. . . .

Please wake up; it is morning;

robins whistle; the bees dance.

Isn't this other one listening

from her shell of silence,

and shouldn't she smile at the green return

and dappled light through windows.

As Earth orbits the corridor

clocks are wound. . . .

The last hour is a song or wound. . . .

Except in this corridor—Mother's—

where finity's brainless wind

blows ash, and ash again

blows through their cells:

So much silence, so little to say in the end.)

Pearly flying hair,

shirt lit with spring flora

and zephyrs, she is a wedding

unto herself. We're leaving

the hall where George jazzes

a piano for the only one dancing.

The others were exhausted

before they arrived,

but she announces the sweetness

of earth and of sky—

she may as well be intoxicated. We like

to say so. It's the purpose

of a wedding.

She is dancing. We won't say

she's dying. George came to her room

to get her, smiled toward us,

we handed her over

in the hall, and then we went

out the front door

whose code

few there remember.

Abandoned bee boxes piled on each other at meadow end . . .

Like clothing taken off,

the bees who had alighted on hat,

gloves, shirt, have flown off somewhere.

Is it so terrible to outlive the mind?

Forget this, forget that—keys, glasses,

what it was you just said, what you meant to say.

Pseudonyms. Silences:

oddball or golden and grave, a dance of signs,

sorrows passing by like shadows,

time running by like a small girl running by like a madwoman.

(*Tyrannus tyrannus*)

That bird towering: late summer

garden: who senses the burring wings

deep inside roses and like the angel

before all nectar's sipped

before gold scatters in bright air

descends from its high height

to lift away the bee . . .

not a honey eater: though looking so:

bee after bee disappearing

into incandescence::

Only the metaphysic flower

feels the approach: and emptying.

(*Ursinus*)

Gold helm scent of honey and the drowsing bear:

golden: begotten of honey: bee larvae

chokeberry sweet clover carrion::

leaving the den in the undergrowth

for sweet-thaw sun-thaw above:

shut out from all the world within:

The valleys and hills feel its feet:

shambling when the sun is low:

slow mouth: Didn't Mother say she felt

its presence a long time?

thought small as atoms,

and aromatic as honey ales:

body manacled—body preserving

small sweetnesses?

until the bear groaned and stretched:

entered there and deeply ate?

I remember the psychiatrist's exam—

Draw a clock.

Hers was a stone sundial,

numbers rubbed away.

Try again, and she quartered the day,

but there were no hands

to lift and drop sunlight

and moon's cold clay.

How exposed she was—

dark, cruel

moment when she found out—

mind a papery hive sliced

open, herself furious.

Then it was autumn.

Each morning she would rise and dress
and walk out the back door where orange rounds
hung from boughs—breasts, big acorns, eggs, jewelry bags?
She waited, she told me, for the right word
to come back to her. Maybe she stood on the patio a few minutes
or hours. The closing click of the door behind her
made her look back, and she stepped inside.
I don't think I believed her then. The weeks passed,
the months, then her forgetfulness blended with angers,
as if red wild bees were knocked from large red blossoms
by witches. When she began her wandering
along cracking pavement, by blank billboards, toward lights
that in the distance must have seemed mythic (or she slept,
intent on making time go away, like a vagrant),
then I felt hushing in her before, by dark severance,
flesh no longer could feed the sweetest mind.
Honeycomb, goddess, death, fate, and the human heart,
they lived in her until too many of her words
flew like birds of the muses away, so few at first
that their disappearance didn't much matter.

Two anthills and a late summer hive

gone to fragments.

The dirt is acrid, the wax honeyed—

so mind makes laws, dividing seasons,

scents, light and light's reflections.

I have no mother. Yes, you have a mother,

a voice said. But that is not right. Her difference—

a broken hive . . . a black bear in the bluebells

clawing the stinging air . . . something torn from her.

Still, the land soothes me—*No one may come—:*

low sun, dusk, and charred trees,

seeming first to glow as they darken, really are only darkening,

as if autumn burned.

And if I want it otherwise, O Self,

there's beauty in small lies.

I say bees lick nectar after dark

and bring it to the bough of the honey tree.

Royal jelly keeps the larvae from falling

from the cells. *Broodcomb, honeycomb, beebread—*

this is a harmless thought. Yes, once I *had* a mother.

I said to her, there is no twenty

on the clock, don't worry. I said

I will tell you the time. She said how little it takes

to finish . . . *What?*

Stupid, Orphean things swirl:

Apricot flowers . . . bees circling

as many times as the distance to the nectar . . .

throbbing wings . . . buzzing . . .

then to pluck the mind from darkness

singing. Mother hears

ambient grief and, more and more,

her earlier German tongue—rhyming, Schiller lines.

Where were you? I'll ask. *Wer bist du,* she'll say,

winter in voices, drifting,

snowdrift, freezing, the bees dropping

to the hardpan inner darkness . . . O Mother . . .

As if by amber or in Lethe's stream

she has been caught, yet still I find it strange

I cannot reach her, who says I look like her.

Where is her mind? A glimmer sometimes forms

as dawn forms on the horizon, but she sorrows

until it's dark again and she no longer knows

that thing from this. The organic

earth and the universe seem themselves to pulse

with Time and leave behind their proofs:

pictured constellations and ancient insects

whose molecules for brain motion

exist in us. We go on living,

this year's renewing sap still untasted

above the heaped decay of last fall

when she first lost her way.

The honeycomb is made from flowers

and the materials for wax bees gather

from the resinous gum of trees,

while honey is distilled from dew.

At the rising of the constellations

or when a rainbow is in the sky,

the dew is deposited in the comb.

Dew from sweet-tasted flowers.

This, Mother, is my song for you

pretending to sleep with open eyes.

As odor and dance lead bees to nectar,

though you're far away I will come to you.

You suddenly wearied. You had to sit

under the sun's force, chilled and sweating,

that hot afternoon in Key West. I think it was 1997.

Your eyes grew very bright. Like two zigzag butterflies,

time and your sense of it spiraled out

over the water. (I'm not sure of the date.)

A ship rumbled in the harbor,

the burning sky was intent on the water.

I'll try to remember the exact date.

You couldn't follow their course

past a certain point, but this was the onset

of your forgetfulness. I told you—Key West in 1997.

What date (not to all, but to you and to me

the year is of importance)? Remember. It was

a hot afternoon in Key West. 1997.

A little problem with space and time, we used to say,

when the diagnosis sounded too harsh.

What year was it, you ask? 1997.

It couldn't have been hotter.

Yes, Key West. No, not honeybees—two butterflies.

You know the year.

1997.

Amid a menagerie she sleeps as in a lair—

lion, bear, and wolf bedded in rich darkness,

the air sweet with opiates—and when she wakes

refreshed, small lights in her clear animal eyes,

it's easy to imagine that the animals have spoken

in a dream of the allegorical life:

Out of the wounded side honey issues.

In light, dementia exposes the sweet lie.

She gazes but rarely speaks—tree names, German

flowers haltingly knot on the string

she once could string without thought.

The question of her being, of whether she was,

insisted on being asked. If once

the beauty in photos

all knew, how could she be

this other—fervorless and gaunt—or wasn't

the mirror cracked? And with the stinging truth

came her need for more and more sleep

in flowered bedclothes, with the animals

with fixed eyes who seemed to have been

waiting for her still sexual scent and weight

to dream them again all into life.

Odor plume, mellifluous humming, thick syrup

made from nectar, calyx: cave of bees—

wild Eden come to this: a room next to a similar room

where women are cared for. *Where are the men?*

my mother asks in a tone suggesting God's interference.

There was one who gardened, his head bent

over a bed of roses; between her and him only a window

patched with glass emblems of stars. She tapped,

he smiled. Then he was sent away, but left for her

a drawing of a horse, pawing with front hooves

the bottom of the yellow page of paper

torn from a notebook; otherwise motionless

as if in amber. Her daughter-in-law taped it to the wall.

She broods on darkness as it seals her room,

then broods on dawn, as if they were the same—

time before the archangel came to punish

when Eve and Adam swayed on Eden's gate

and couldn't yet leave.

It was August, it was August

and she was dancing, no, we three were dancing.

Her paranoia wasn't yet Thracian.

I thought of the greenhouse in Vienna,

my grandmother, her mother, dancing

while her partner's wife sat stone-lipped

among roses in the Viennese greenhouse.

I was young, what do the young know

of forgivable sin? I was stone-lipped.

My husband was singing, while dancing,

his sin his innocence—how old must one be to know

that sexual beauty is dangerous at any age?

My husband sang "Embraceable You" and danced,

Mother dipped toward him, and he turned

to her. She'd want to tear him to pieces,

but she didn't know that

until in the end he spurned her—

her mind jangled like bees in a sac.

But she didn't know that.

It was August, it was only August.

If her falling to quiet

after harsh years reversed, where
would it start if not before irony,
hurt, want, sex?
Time's soft machine goes past
spring, and last, past
Lascaux and the first magnifications
on stone, before the first look in a pool
the first I am, and back
before tongues licked
nectar, wings fanning honey, and body
carrying sexual powders
through conifer forests
to begin the abominable diversification
of flowers:: to rain,
to one drop crashing.

To live without memory is to have each hour

as a pane of air for canvas and the view from a window

to paint: amber-honey cold mornings:

humbled by evening: variation and variation

of ambiguous figments—ziggurat beehive

auroras—flicker and go out. All history

may as well be in these brushstrokes:

the hand has not rested nor the paint dried.

As small lamps drift with river tide

and against the wind, her reverie keeps wavering,

her gaze inward. Beyond is the dark, chopped bay,

beyond no lights at all. Couldn't she step

ashore to a place with its own name

and return, knowing the difference

between there and here? She has told me

of the sea in legendary depth and darkness,

the moon's huge black bulk, apparitional

salt lilies in the blind valleys of the ocean's floor,

brain blots—no stars at all, no, no

spindrift light, no nearness

that in sudden whirlpool

doesn't sink and cease to remember.

Beauty and dust, beauty and dust—

but to simplify we say dementia

(time sensing, recognizing, recollecting

soon ceasing), not imagine the fields along Lethe

dim lit but with their few flowers: corolla

and grains of pollen for the ancient bees.

A little problem with space

and time, she and I first kidded,

is becoming no place and perilous travel,

days harsher than mineral. Lethe

is someplace. Water laps against

a wooden boat. In time of frankness, lie.

Tell her she will come soon with you home.

All things are taken from us

and in a little while our cares
are numb. Lotus pollen wafts
through the valleys and shadows.

Our bodies outlast us, sleep—
wandering in the spiced mist,
even as we sit. We sip the cup
if it is offered. Is it milk?

To taste would be
a simple perfection of thought—
the brain's wild bee that grows
honey seeking bee rose.

Swollen with dust and rain
and rumor, our eyes grow inward.
It is restful knowing nothing
more, knowing no one any more.

The mind is no tunnel deepening

to a pent element, perhaps an underground lake
of undrinkable waters,
bottom silted over
with names of objects and the people
she has known all her life. She can recite
"Die Lorelei" and recognizes the Dalai Lama
but not you. Sure, you want to know how
she can talk politics and laugh
but not ladle up a family memory.
It helps to read a book,
change her prescription,
see in her clouded eyes
breezes of light,
think of the myth of the mantis,
who in its exhaustion was laid
on a floating flower. In its thigh
a seed was left, the bee flew on,
all people came to life,
and nothing yet themselves
drank minutes shut in the water.
"Why am I here?" they asked,
and answered then, "To see what comes,

beginning first faintly to look like

something, some parts missing,

fish fins, for instance. We *almost* see it:

turning into gilly, or red butterfly

in water, on black sand. Crisp gills,

insect petals, rose-red, and the even darker,

accurate rose of blood. Then words

rooted at the bottom of the lake,

or agitating the heart."

Said so (their heads dripping with water),

it will be hard to turn away.

But remember the woman

in her dementia who is half dead.

The myth is too pretty.

"Generous I may have been, amnesiac

I became. Autumn fattened and thinned;

I stared at the clock's senseless hands.

I let the girl in the market make change.

I looked at my lists of medicines

and the bottles on the shelf, but they

seemed separate. In the bathroom mirror

my face was suddenly antediluvian who

was I? I'd be thinking and at the first touch

of attention, I'd forget. I cut my own hair.

I saw my mother wrapped in a mantilla

in her coffin. Why did I find my skin's

imperfections so interesting and pick off

moles? If I went to the end of the street,

would I be at the center of myself?

Insects watched me. They got in my hair.

I'd be at the opera house in Vienna.

The planes strafed the Strassenbahn.

My hands fluttered then like butterflies.

For a little while I knew—there was a door,

a split in the wall, and I was two persons,

old and young, wise and clean, sturdy and

bent, generous and dead. They were

neck on neck like winter and spring

but could do nothing for each other.

I'm leaving, I know, each said,

a flooding darkness in their eyes,

a drawing down of blinds. Afterward

my feelings were the eyes of moths.

They . . . What is the word between eyes

and too little light? I knew. I think so.

Meanings fissured. Words hollowed.

It was like the thing with bees—

I swatted in front of my face

and hated them. Then there were none."

Light clear in a window, morning

finding white flowers, herself climbing

in the Alps alone to the meadow

of edelweiss and descending

at dusk—rock and field slurring. . . .

In her corner room she sleeps and grieves,

bedclothes like dirty plumage.

Light and lamp now drug her.

She was the child Sorrow

in *Madama Butterfly.*   Staatsoper

Haus.   Bombs, strafing,

gut of some war? Where are stones

that were her city?

Who kissed her?

I want to hear those stories,

but she may as well be lyre

and head on a black river, singing

to no one.

A hundred answers within her burn.

When I (*You look like me who are you?*) tell her

the words Marlene Dietrich,

the Marlene she loves, sings,

the melody won't coax the hours.

Her mind's a bedraggled swan on a black river.

Why are we here who owns this house

she asks: The dark place she thinks is

an ocean at 3 A.M.: no stars or moon:

She's swimming alone.

Chocolate dribbles to her chin:

We feed her chocolate because

she likes chocolate and she

forgets *Who owns this house Why* . . .

We walk in her garden:

We hold on to her elbows: Here's the fruit

honey fungus in the hive

where we all may end our days—

anonymous, named. . . . Ought not

to make elegies out of our fear

but we do. Yesterdays wilt:

the smoke for calming

bees drifts to our heads::

Why are we here in this state:

the landscape flowing away: tides

disturbing the shore?

Whoever comes after can gather

those bumping on the disturbed shore.

The humble sense of being alive

under the towering sun

fills the nectary and ripens apricots

down to the last one,

if Mnemosyne wakens from apathy

each moment. It is the soft burly sound

of a bee tumbled in fritillary,

is it not?

But if memory, as if to illustrate

the mind was not yours to have,

the mind was not given,

fails us, leaving us in our underpants

in the garden, should we not

hate the garden,

or the woman whose garden

it is? And sunlight. Thunder.

Rain. Hardened in heart against

what Earth compels and seizes,

god damning, god damned rain.

Pretty to think of the mind at its end

as a metaphysician beekeeping

after the leaves have fallen at autumn's end:

Never sweeter, closer, those hours

before the pears fell. Were not the cells and stars

fruit-smelling? Where are those hours?

In the ashes of old pains and joys, in the burning

and nectar, the interstellar black garden,

the cold solstice, space inside a space once burning.

❊

The wintriest gray shape, beauty

smoked out—no longer full of rapture, sweet lies

(See, the beekeeper's terrible blank eyes are trying

to make whoever looks see that he no longer knows

what to think, do, feel, or even what day it is, and he succeeds.)—

but a blunt empty box.

I see the unmarked snow,

the yawning tree, shriveled bees

on the bottom pan, and I see dead beauty.

She wears geegaws from relatives

who smile when she tells of thieves

coming with any change of light,

when she drowses late or leaves her room early.

She has hidden and can't find her amethyst

and rain sapphire.

There was the gold necklace

she wore as naturally as a sun bear's golden bib,

the clasp so strong the thief in the subway

a world ago couldn't break it,

dragging her along the platform

as if along the dark ramparts

of a besieged city.

Where, now, has that been put?

Old, did Helen wear diadems?

Did she know glass from diamonds?

Her daughter-in-law admires the box ribbon

wound around her wrist. She smiles

and winds her bracelet once more

with little apprehension

of small evils and lies.

I'll give it to you, she says. *Later on.*

She saw that the tortured dream wrestled to the floor

was a gray-haired woman. She saw

the walls and connecting corridors of Legacy Heights

as prison, and when the nurses phoned her son,

he took away her telephone as punishment

for hallucination. She knew this for a few days,

then forgot. *Were her fantasies*

drug-induced? I asked the staff. They looked

at each other. I asked my brother. He said,

Why isn't she able to rejoice with joyous dreams?

Why is she so negative? Irremediable, the being

in two worlds, one leg in Lethe,

the other in a leaden Styx, I countered,

but only in my quiet, reprimanding,

the yellow asp stinging the black heart.

That was the mind's wild swarm trapezing from an oak limb,

odor of honey and blue sky ablaze—until the regress.
Only what's inmost is left and darkened past language,
and she is like a tiny star that Space no longer notices,
unillumined, hushed, and by herself, her course no longer
in the scheme of planets, suns, and lunar systems.
But she is still here. What breaks the archetypal
stone and starves the honeybees moves toward her slowly.

When bees sicken a rough

leanness or fat mars their appearance: all listless and silent::

Give them honey through straws, freely calling them

and exhorting them to eat their familiar foods

and swallow the Aricept.

But if they fail, may as well say prepare

the hide of a bull with thyme and fresh rosemary

so moisture, warming in the softened bone, ferments—

and without feet at first, but soon with whirring wings as well,

more and more try the clear air, until they burst out

like rain pouring from cumulus clouds,

or arrows from twanging bows (bees are the bowstring).

Then the queen revives.

She doesn't see herself in the mirror,

the mind's white rum

spilt, cosmos a thimble:

When we're diminished to this,

when stars are granular,

candying a thimble of

brain cells, how will we

care? I tell her there are two

of us there in

the mirror, two

faces there. She says no,

I see you, I'm not there.

You'll ask if she smiled

or blinked when she said so. No.

Fools die every day they live

And in death, as in sleep,

thought no longer clings to Earth's

cool granite. There could be

a wild child and a peacock drinking

themselves from a pool

that agitates in gold and rainbow.

There could be a hell of stars.

In daylight, Earth's foot

on their necks, minds ravined

by bees, seasons slowing,

the chalk of their bones softening,

hunchbacked, lost,

emotions strewn,

they listen for the roar of death

to take them to one last

brilliant destination—

flame swerve of ten thousand

candles in that big a wind.

Erring   shoe and sour bib

her dress, wild hair, the woman

is following the turning path.

About her, attendants in white

in a parallel world   wait.

One keeps the drug cart.

One writes on palimpsest

of another fretting mind.

They have not brought her

or kept her from the clamorous

     world to the labyrinth,

whose entrance   is age,

for reprimand though she feels

it, but simply

to give her a place freely   to move

past season and sun and change

inside coded doors   and honeyed

paneling. At the center

is the courtyard for activity.

Tuesdays a piano plays

and all may dance.

It is no more joyous for them

or for the family until

having walked so long among

the turnings, she loses sense

of direction and all trace

of what it was like before.

It is not easy to be free

forever of a wish never

to go back instead to whirl naked

in a bare world.

What makes her quiet

when they hand her a doll?
What is the doll to her? She's no fool
in this old colony
where half can't wipe up
after themselves. She must know
this May morning in the enclosed
courtyard, a tree white-veiled,
there's no return
to a day when Mother
takes her first up in arms.

The doll is naked.
She sees that and maybe hears
inside her head someone crooning,
someone else she can't name.
It's hard to ask her. Her hair is loosened,
her blouse food-bedabbled,
and she no longer apprehends
or doesn't mind the murderous stealth
of shade just starting to break
a bough. Now, *now,*
let her rock her doll.

I watched her sleep then went to the window.

Morning light—cool, honey-hungry—

kept vigil in the garden,

and I thought, The gigantic mind that is suddenly

consumed is not less planetary. Star, stone-rooted

rose, and the winds speak paradise,

speak grave. Knowing this turned me back

to her with final calm.

Afterword

From the somber deeps horseshoe crabs crawled up on somber shores:

Man-of-wars' blue sails drifted downwind

and blue filaments of some biblical clock

floated below: the stinging filaments:

The cored of bone and rock-headed came near:

Clouds made wandering shadows:

Sea and grasses mingled::

There was no hell after all

but a lull before it began over::

flesh lying alone: then mating: a little spray of soul:

and the grace of waves, of stars, and remotest isles.

Carol Frost is the author of ten previous collections of poems, including *The Queen's Desertion, I Will Say Beauty,* and *Love and Scorn* from North-western University Press. She has received National Endowment for the Arts fellowships and PEN and Pushcart awards, and she has been honored by the Elliston and the Poets' Prize committees. She holds the Theodore Bruce and Barbara Lawrence Alfond Chair of English at Rollins College, where she directs the Winter with the Writers Literary Festival.

green
press
INITIATIVE

Northwestern University Press is committed to preserving ancient forests and natural resources. We elected to print this title on 30% post consumer recycled paper, processed chlorine free. As a result, for this printing, we have saved:

1 Trees (40' tall and 6-8" diameter)
560 Gallons of Wastewater
1 Million BTUs of Total Energy
34 Pounds of Solid Waste
116 Pounds of Greenhouse Gases

Northwestern University Press made this paper choice because our printer, Thomson-Shore, Inc., is a member of Green Press Initiative, a nonprofit program dedicated to supporting authors, publishers, and suppliers in their efforts to reduce their use of fiber obtained from endangered forests.

For more information, visit www.greenpressinitiative.org

Environmental impact estimates were made using the Environmental Defense Paper Calculator. For more information visit: www.papercalculator.org.